SELF-PORTRAIT IN A DOOR-LENGTH MIRROR

2017 winner
MILLER WILLIAMS
poetry prize

SELF-PORTRAIT IN A

DOOR-LENGTH MIRROR

POEMS BY STEPHEN GIBSON

The University of Arkansas Press
Fayetteville
2017

Once again, for my wife Clo,
my daughter Kyla, and my son Joe

And once again in memory of
my mother Mary Agnes and my father Russell

Series Editor's Preface

Miller Williams was the first editor to spot me, you might say, and subsequently, the one who published my first full-length book of poems, *The Apple That Astonished Paris,* in 1988. With a single stroke, I was transformed into a "published poet," an all-too-common phrase that reminds us of the vast number of poets who are unpublished, or as an optimist might say, "pre-published." Funny, we don't hear much about "unpublished novelists" or "unpublished journalists."

Since then, I have felt a special debt to Miller for the validation he gave me and for the delicacy with which he edited that collection. "You have a line that goes, 'I can see it so clearly.' I don't think you need that intensifier '*so*,'" he told me in our first talk on the phone. I was left with the feeling that this man had read my poems more closely and carefully than I had. I won't forget that initial phone call. Miller happened to find me in a hotel in Miami, where I was getting dressed to go to Hialeah for a day at the races. When I heard him say he was going to publish my book, I knew I'd been granted more than enough luck for one day; it was a pleasure to spend the afternoon losing one race after another. I wasn't just someone who couldn't pick a winner; I was a *published poet* who couldn't pick a winner. The day was made even better because my best pal was with me, and we even ran into Carol Flake, whose horse book, *Tarnished Crown,* was just about to be published.

Judging this prize, which is named in honor of the cofounder and director of the University of Arkansas Press, gives me the opportunity to pass on the gift that Miller Williams gave to me, the publication of a book of poems, in some cases a first book. For a poet, in terms of sheer thrills, there is no publication that matches his or her first book. With all this in mind, it follows that serving as judge for the Miller Williams Poetry Prize is great pleasure for me.

Even if one is so blissfully egalitarian and nonjudgmental as to believe that all poetry manuscripts are equal, one must concede that some are more equal than others. This year, all of the "more equal" ones were eye-openers for me, literary wake-up calls that brought me to attention, each for a very different reason.

Self-Portrait in a Door-Length Mirror might be an intentional echo of Ashbery's convex mirror, but Stephen Gibson's language is neither coy nor elliptical as Ashbery's typically is. Instead, Gibson presents a series of clear formalist poems, each organized around a different kind of patterning. A series of 8 seven-line poems—each in the rectangular shape of a painting—examines the life and art of Pierre Bonnard. But the focus is Marthe de Méligny, Bonnard's lover, model, and eventually, his wife. The eroticism of Marthe washing her feet in a bathtub or being submerged in it naked is balanced by the mention of the objects in the painting where "everything alive . . . is dead." Add to this grouping an intricately successful pantoum about Diane Arbus, along with my favorite, a twenty-seven-line monorhyme (a tour de force, by the way) written in reaction to a photograph of Hermann Göring's suicide. The radical subjects of Arbus (also a suicide) and SS Commander Göring are brought under control by the imposition of form. The resulting tension shows this exceptional poet at his rhyming best.

Mr. Stevens' Secretary—yes, it's *that* Mr. Stevens—is a series of vignettes taken from (or invented to create) the life of the great modernist's secretary. We see what Stevens looked like from her point of view, which includes how Stevens smelled—not bad as it turns out: "Oriental . . . but that may be that was because of the tea . . . White peony tea." A mild eroticism builds when we are told that the secretary keeps a special bottle of Chantilly "not at home but in her desk." We also get to see the secretary outside of her job in a poem about wasps and marriage and another about her pre-Stevens employers. But it is the famous poet who cannot distinguish *its* from *it's*. In another poem, she attempts to write a fable in which a father saves a cat who got its head stuck in a milk bottle, yet he has an awful temper and shouts "horribly" at his wife. Like Carol Ann Duffy's boldly feminist collection, *The World's Wife,* Frances Schenkkan's *Mr. Stevens' Secretary* forces readers to adjust their perspective by showing a great man through the eyes of a previously silent and less visible woman.

One requirement for poets is the ability to write about two different things at the same time. Seamus Heaney turns writing into a kind of digging. John Ciardi intertwines marriage and the structure of an arch. Among the several poems in Jennifer Givhan's *Protection Spell* that stopped me cold is "The Polar Bear," in which a mother tries to protect her black child from the television news of racial unrest (riots, arrests, brutality) by turning his attention to the Discovery Channel. But there, a polar bear is fighting for survival surrounded by vicious walruses and melting ice. The boy clutches his stuffed white bear and asks if this is real. Life in the Arctic and life in the urban streets are conjoined, ecology and racism wed. Givhan is a poet of great heart and brave directness who writes real life poems, sometimes crowded to the point of claustrophobia with the details of life in the poor lane. One poem transforms a laundromat woman living "paycheck to paycheck" into a "god." Another poem is a stirring defense of cheerleaders, written without a drop of irony. A reader will be quick to trust the authority in this poet's voice and the credentials of experience that are on full display.

Not all the poems in *The Wild Night Dress* by Laura McCullough use scientific or technological language, but many of them do, and in ways that create interesting effects. This poet has the kind of binocular vision that can see the poetic and scientific aspects of the world simultaneously. The poem "Feed" opens: "In a drone video of Humpbacks / feeding off the coast of Canada, / the surface of the ocean is frothed into blossoms." The ending of that last line returns the poem to poetry's musical origins without implying any friction between this lovely sound and drone technology. In a poem in which the speaker hungers for eggs, this mix of diction occurs: "though I wish to fill myself, / until the ventromedial hypothalamus [the gland that stimulates hunger] / is so stimulated / all I can think of is flowers." This shuffling together of lyrical/botanical and medical language is done so gracefully, it has the effect of bringing "the two cultures" into a rare state of peaceful coexistence. Also engaging are the more traditionally lyric poems, one about childhood, another about a "fawn caught in the family compost" (for me, an echo of the cat caught in a milk bottle in *Mr. Stevens' Secretary*), but the distinction this collection can best claim is the way the poems find an easy synthesis between poetry and science. Perhaps Laura McCullough's most telling confession lies in this couplet: "I can't help loving / the word *sonoluminescence.*"

I'm glad that early on, the editors at the press and I agreed that the judge for these prizes should not be looking for poems that sound like the poems of Miller Williams but for poems that Miller might have enjoyed and admired. It's easy for me to picture Miller paging through these four books with a look of appreciation and even delight on his face, though he might keep a red pencil nearby just in case he comes across one of those annoying, unnecessary "intensifiers."

Billy Collins

Acknowledgments

Grateful acknowledgments are made to the editors of the following magazines in which these poems, or earlier versions of them, first appeared:

Copper Nickel: "Improvisation on Warhol's *Campbell's Soup Cans*"

Gargoyle Magazine: "Saving the Mare"

Lake Effect: "Sacred Flesh: Bonnard"

Mid-American Review: "On Guido Reni's *Apollo Flaying Marsyas* as Iraq"

nd[re]view: "Genghis Khan in Chicago"

New Madrid: "Crossing Sartre's Bridge with Inez and Estelle during the Iraq War"

North American Review: "Crime Scene Photo of a Hotel Murder in the Times Square Area" and "Apocalypse"

Per Contra: "In Memoriam C. E. 1957–2014" and "Nudes"

Pleiades: "Chickpeas" and "Chickpeas"

River Styx: "1957"

Salamander: "X-Factors: De Chirico"

Shenandoah: "Craigslist Killer Noir" and "Manhattan Noir"

Southern Humanities Review: "View of the Paris Communard Dead Murdered by Versailles Troops at Père-Lachaise Cemetery, 1871"

Southwest Review: "Diane Arbus: Self-Portrait in a Door-Length Mirror"

Superstition Review: "Variations on a Simile Overheard at a Showing of Quentin Tarantino's *Django Unchained*"

"Megapixels" originally appeared in *River Styx*, no. 84, 2011, selected by Maxine Kumin as winner of the 2010 *River Styx* International Poetry Contest.

"Girl by a Window" originally appeared in the *Southern Review*, vol. 48, no. 4, autumn 2012.

"Boxes," "A Pipe," and "'60s Fellini Noir" first appeared in the *Notre Dame Review*, no. 36, Summer/Fall 2013.

"Nuremberg" was first published in the *Sewanee Review*, vol. 122, no. 2, spring 2014. Copyright 2014 by Stephen Gibson.

"Looking at the Göring Suicide Photograph" was first published in the *Yale Review*, vol. 103, no. 3, July 2015.

"Lewis Carroll Photographs of Alice Liddell" was first published in the *Sewanee Review*, vol. 124, no. 4, fall 2016. Copyright 2016 by Stephen Gibson.

Thanks to my brother Tim and to my lifelong friend Ed Falco. Thanks to the many poets whose works have enriched my life. Thanks also to everyone at the University of Arkansas Press for their care, expertise, and excellence. A special thanks to Billy Collins.

Contents

SELF-PORTRAIT IN A DOOR-LENGTH MIRROR

Diane Arbus: Self-Portrait in a Door-Length Mirror

Why would I ever want to bring you
into this world? To one day take your place
among the ordinary misfits I view
all around me and record face to face?

One day in this world, they take your place
and you're not even aware it's happened,
but all around me I record it, face to face,
those who will survive me when I'm dead.

But you're not even aware it's happened
because you're just a small bump in the mirror
who will inevitably survive me when I'm dead,
trying to come to terms with you and her—

her (me) looking at the bump in the mirror
of you, photographing it, the panty elastic
lowered to define, like a horizon, you from her
that I became aware of like a twitch, a tic.

I was examining a panty-tear at the elastic
and was going to throw them out, but didn't.
That's when I felt something, a twitch, a tic.
I knew somehow something was different.

I was going to throw them out, but I didn't.
And here you are, with me in the apartment,

knowing everything and nothing is different
as I photograph you without your consent.

Forgive me bringing you into this apartment,
telling you all of these things that I shouldn't,
for photographing you without your consent,
for not knowing why I did something, or didn't.

Like saying all of these things that I shouldn't.
Life is difficult enough from whatever view
not knowing why you shot something or didn't,
like, at this moment, in this world, shooting you.

I

Genghis Khan in Chicago

I'm at the AWP conference in Chicago.
This morning I was headed for a fiction panel. I didn't go.

I went to the Field Museum to see the exhibition on Genghis Khan.
The museum is geared toward families with children.

I knew what to expect—photos of contemporary Mongols eating
        yoghurt
beside the opening to an actual, collapsible yurt

that kids walked through with their parents.
A children's history of Mongol warfare. Not murder. Not rape.
      It makes sense.

To this day babies are born in eastern Europe with a blue smear
at the tip of their spines, like ink spreading on blotting paper.

It's a recessive trait that goes back to those Mongols.
My niece, who's adopted from southern Russia, has it, so I know.

The bar stools are filled with young MFA students out having fun.
I'm at a table in Kitty O'Sheas eating shepherd's pie, and telling
      this to no one.

Girl by a Window

Venice

The staff girl was sitting by a window, looking
    out to a courtyard below, a museum brochure
absentmindedly fanning her throat. Sweaty,

the girl pulled her dark gray-and-blue uniform-
    blouse away from her breasts, which shone
with perspiration. I watched her in the dark.

She didn't notice me. She sat there in the dark
    on a folding chair, floor fan not working, looking
outside through the window as if she'd been shown

something and was still looking for it, her brochure
    fanning as she absently pinched her uniform
away from her breasts. Even the paintings were sweaty.

There was no air-conditioning. Their canvases—sweaty
    with humidity—cracked out of their huge, dark,
carved frames. As soldiers with pikes and metal uniforms

slaughtered each other, that young girl sat looking
    away, completely uninterested, her museum brochure
fanning her, her attention elsewhere, as if she'd been shown

something and wasn't interested in how swords shone
    against helmets and cuirasses in the bloody, sweaty
grips of dead men. The floor fan was broken. Her brochure

was her fan. She was using it to fan herself in the dark,
	probably dreading that some old guy like me, looking
for some particular painting, would spot her in her uniform

and expect her help. She'd have to button up her uniform
	and try to appear cheerful. Earlier, I'd been shown
by a much-older female guide just what I'd been looking

for, the so-called Bridge of Sighs that led prisoners to sweaty
	dungeons below the waterline of this current-day, dark
and air-conditionless museum where a girl fanning a brochure

looked as trapped as any poor prisoner identified in the brochure
	she was fanning herself with, wanting to take that uniform
off, throw it into a hamper, shower, nap, and then, in the dark

go out, but not into this museum of a city, but to where lights shone
	like stars across the blackness of the lagoon, and the sweaty
canvases of the dead could be left behind as she went looking

for what the young don't have to be shown in any brochure,
	which wears a different uniform, which is sweaty and vibrant
in the dark and finds itself looking out through a different window.

1957

That evening, tears flowed. Under the astonished gaze
of the congregants spilling out of the humble church
(which had to close its doors to those outside on its steps—
and beyond) prayers rose into the blackest black night has.

Every one of the congregants inside the humble church
saw a crimson teardrop flow down the cheek of the Virgin.
From a plaster statue. Prayers rose into the black of night.
This miracle happened in winter in New Mexico in 1957.

They saw a crimson tear flow down the cheek of the Virgin.
This happened during the rosary after the doors closed.
New Mexico, cold, winter, 1957—the miracle happened.
Only much later did a janitor confess to creating the hoax.

During the rosary after the doors were closed in the church,
pig fat on one cheek began to melt; the food coloring, to run.
Only much later did the janitor confess to creating the hoax.
He didn't explain why he did it; he described only what he did.

He applied pig fat to a cheek, with food coloring, which ran
when the body-heat of the congregants filled up the church.
He didn't explain why he did it; he described only what he did.
Like blood, a red tear formed on the Virgin's cheek; she wept.

When the body-heat of the congregants filled up the church,
all eyes turned toward the statue in its niche beside the altar:
a blood tear running down the Virgin's cheek. She was weeping.
It happened again on another night during mass. People wept.

Later, eyes turned toward the statue high up beside the altar
to see if it would happen again—the three networks filmed
to see if it would happen again during mass as people wept.
It didn't, there was nothing to film, then the janitor confessed.

No one would see it happen again as the networks filmed.
This was February. By October, a new moon was in the sky—
the janitor's confession, forgotten; the networks showed film.
The moon weighed 184.3 pounds. It was called Sputnik.

One month later, another new moon launched into the sky—
Sputnik II—inside it was a dog named Laika that was filmed.
In America, some people froze into statutes, hearing the news.
At night, some looked up to the heavens, astonished. Some wept.

Variations on a Simile Overheard at a Showing of Quentin Tarantino's *Django Unchained*

Freud

People are like frogs: desperate, lonely, calling out in darkness
and always being answered in a swamp, but at such distance
they don't know in which direction to turn, and on the chance
they'll turn in a wrong direction, they're overwhelmed by stasis.

Einstein

In the cosmic swamp voices are answered but at distances
so great galaxies blink in and out of existence like fireflies
and to turn in any direction is to be overwhelmed by stasis;
that is, by the illusion that appearance is permanent by design.

Hawking

The universe is not blinking in and out of existence like a firefly,
or, if it is, it is a firefly about to be snatched out by a frog's tongue
and everything that appears to be permanent is an illusion by design
in mathematics, to one day end, like a firefly's light, in total darkness.

Bishop Sheen

If existence is a firefly about to be snatched out by a frog's tongue
then humanism has reached its nadir begun with the Renaissance:
mathematics may prove time, like a firefly, will blink out in darkness
but can never disprove another existence after what it calls the end.

Stalin

That humanism since the Renaissance has reached a low point
may be true but it is also irrelevant, and even that article of faith
cannot disprove another existence for what some deny is the end
but a bullet to the forehead confirms for most the end is the end.

Camus

Everything is true/untrue, relevant/irrelevant, an article of faith
and a product of humanity's disbelief that at the core is nothing,
that the end is end, which comes for most like a bullet to the head,
which, in turn, demands disproof, making affirmation possible.

Cotton Mather

We are the product of humanity's disbelief; at our core is nothing.
If I have a toothache, it is because I've willfully sinned in my teeth.
God's wrath is severe and, in the end, will be as a bullet to the head:
inevitable, inescapable, unstoppable, indescribable, effectual, and final.

Sartre

In the ache of the September 11th firefighter finding a tooth is Being,
the human, but not as frog, desperate, alone, calling out in darkness.
In that moment he knows the inevitable, inescapable, unstoppable;
his turning in any direction to hold on to something is Nothingness.

Crime Scene Photo of a Hotel Murder in the Times Square Area

One said it was the same as walking into a hotel
room that wasn't yet made up for the new guests:
there was floss on a tampon wrapper in the basket
in the bathroom; there was a half-empty water bottle.

The room wasn't yet made up for its new guests;
that would come after the cops finished with her
and the bathroom and the half-empty water bottle
on the nightstand beside the yellow to-do pad.

The cop in the bathroom wasn't finished with her,
and with a latex glove picked up the piece of floss.
On the nightstand the yellow to-do pad was blank
and the cop there wondered if she had a to-do list,

like the cop picking up the piece of floss wondered
how you could floss one minute and be dead the next.
The nightstand cop wondered about the blank to-do list.
She had one—this was New York—she was a tourist,

but you could floss one minute and be dead the next.
She looked like a pretend dead *Vogue* model in an ad
some big-shot agency set in New York so the tourists
would buy the perfume and feel their lives dangerous.

Wearing black lace underwear, like the *Vogue* model,
she wasn't pretending she was dead, because she was.
You could buy the perfume or not, life's dangerous.
That's the way it is—death doesn't go on vacation.

Unlike the model pretending to be dead, she was.
Just a pretty woman in New York, with her period.
That's the way it was—death doesn't go on vacation
and killers don't take one because you're on one,

just a pretty woman in New York with your period,
looking like you could be a *Vogue* model in an ad.
Killers don't take a vacation because you're on one.
If Warhol were still around, there'd be a lithograph

of the scene (later copied by some *Vogue* model ad)
including the floss on the tampon wrapper in the basket.
SoHo would throw a party for Warhol's new lithographs,
everyone believing life wasn't half as dangerous as art.

Manhattan Noir

She played in a philharmonic; he was a handyman.
She was trained how to hold a cello by the neck
and draw a bow across its strings so that sound
made listeners leave this world and find themselves
in another that for most was impossible to express.
He strangled her to death backstage behind a curtain.

Her disappearance from other's lives was like a curtain
suddenly being pulled across in front of them, a woman
who was so talented and alive. How do you express
what the loss of such a gift is, they asked. Her neck
was crushed. That's what people repeated to themselves
when her murder was discovered, and without sound

they attended her memorial, and, except for the sound
of their own breathing, they stared at a stage curtain
with a large photograph of her which they themselves
recognized as if they had taken it of that young woman,
which showed her smiling, holding her cello by the neck.
Then they left, entered the subway, and took the express

uptown to parts of Manhattan—but even the express
could not take them away fast enough from a sound
that was only absence. He pressed down on her neck
with his thumbs as he knelt over her behind the curtain,
until her eyes almost burst out of her, a young woman
that he admitted not knowing. Family asked themselves,

why? Why did he have to kill her? They themselves
knew the answer—because he could. Because, to express
whatever was inside him, he strangled a young woman
he didn't know but saw at times rehearsing in a sound-
proof rehearsal room. So he hid behind a thick curtain
hiding old lighting equipment. He grabbed her neck,

he admitted to police, and couldn't believe that her neck
was actually between his fingers. His fingers themselves
seemed actually not to have any feeling, as if a curtain
had come between them and her. It was hard to express
what he felt at that moment, even as he heard the sound
coming from her throat as he choked that young woman.

In black dress, she holds the cello's neck, trying to express
not only what great musicians themselves hear, but a sound
she believes lies waiting behind a curtain in every human.

He hid their panties in the back of his closet, trophies
of his attacks (which he didn't think of as attacks),
replayed in his head how everything went down,
not as he planned (nothing ever went as planned),
but had gone well enough, so that on the hospital
ward, making rounds, he could enjoy the moment

though he could never speak about the moment.
At least, out loud. And never about his trophies.
Med students didn't keep trophies. At the hospital
he was one person. EMTs brought in heart attacks,
drug ODs, botched suicides that didn't go as planned
(one jumper caught a hotel canopy on the way down,

enough to slow his speed, though not a tube down
his throat after what should have been a moment
of impact, and then nothing). His fiancée planned
one future for her doctor-squeeze—he was a trophy
for her and knew it and liked it. That man attacks
sex escorts at night after his shifts at the hospital?

You've got to be kidding—he worked at a hospital.
But he knew of a surgeon who was on the down-
low in men's bathrooms—and was once attacked
when he approached the wrong dude, a moment
the surgeon tried to blow off to police. (His trophies
were a wife of thirty years and three kids—that plan

didn't exactly go as Mr. Down-Low had planned,
now did it?) When he wasn't the face at the hospital,
he was someone else, someone who kept trophies
from rooms where he watched them pull them down—
they still smelled of that particular, delicious moment.
Money wasn't the issue (newspapers said the attacks

were escort robberies gone bad). No person attacks
a human being solely for money—and no one plans
what's really going on inside their head at that moment.
But it's going on inside. You see that in the hospital,
the raw essentialness of it   that something deep down
in the other person rising to the surface. That trophy.

The pupils of the heart attack looking back in the hospital.
The surgery not going as planned, the widow sitting down.
The moment everyone will one day come to. That trophy.

Chickpeas
–for Ed Falco

Pimentos. The red of pimentos. The pimentos
in olives—Ed, when you called, I was riding the el
and then feeling up my girlfriend under a stairwell.
Actually, when the phone rang, I was picking
the pimentos out of my olives and feeding the olives
to Joseph who'd climbed on my lap. But what noise

the brain hears, neuron to neuron, when the noise,
we think, is only about olives (with no pimentos)—
not the Bronx—and picturing chickpeas, not olives.
I remembered something I'd forgotten—not the el,
but an old man going through an antipasto, picking
out a chickpea—a life lesson, like under a stairwell,

that Verdi turned into opera (not me under a stairwell
with my girl—but Sicily—with the background noise
of a Bronx restaurant). My friend and I were picking
through olives stuffed with anchovies (not pimentos),
peppers, salami, prosciutto—with the screeching el
outside—when the owner sat. He moved aside olives

and held up a chickpea. *What's this?* he asked. *No olives—
this?* My friend was grinning (the wrought-iron stairwell
behind him was full of people rushing up to catch the el).
Chickpea, I said. He smiled, said something, but the noise

of the train drowned him out. Then he squeezed a pimento
out of an olive. *Franchiski*, he said. My friend was picking

up cheese, then guffawing. (I felt the old man was picking
on me and I didn't know why.) *Oliva*, he said, for an olive—
Ciciri, for the chickpeas. My friend squeezed out a pimento,
repeating *Franchiski*. He was in tears. (Outside, the stairwell
was empty. The restaurant was almost empty. The only noise
was my friend guffawing—the waitress, as if waiting for the el,

looking over from her post. I wanted to leave, take the el
back to my house and never go back there—not picking
up on the allusion both of them were sharing—the noise
of centuries, notwithstanding—about chickpeas, not olives—
involving a married woman, but not under a stairwell
in the Bronx—in 13*th* century Sicily—the red of the pimento

in an olive like a slaughtered French body stuffed in a barrel—
husbands picking their moment, waiting in alleys, under stairwells—
the noise, the screams, the sight of flesh opening red as pimentos.)

Chickpeas
—for Ed Falco

By 1282, Sicily had so long been under the boot of oppressors, this
time the French, the mere look of a foreigner became an insult—
not that husbands didn't know some wives, on occasion, were
more than flattered—as were some daughters—but suspicion only
increased the tension spouses felt toward each other, making the
ordinary life impossible, the oppression worse. "Se non piu sposa,
non piu famiglia," the owner said in the restaurant, and my friend
translated, "Without the wife, there is no family"—the corners of
the old man's mouth turned down. He shook his head. Then he
made a gesture.

"The sign of the horn—the cuckold—a husband whose wife is
cheating," my friend explained—

then the old man's hand slammed down!

"Moranu li Franchiski," the old man shouted (my friend tried
to keep up—"'Death to the French'—too fast—he's talking in
dialect—something about 'the boil erupted'—something about an
official touching a woman outside a church").

Ed, I'd gone into the restaurant with my friend intending to have
a slice of pizza, not a course in food as history, cultural memory,
or the collective unconscious. I couldn't understand one half
he said. To make a long story short, the old man explained how
women who'd fraternized with the French garrison now tried to

plead for their lovers—and then later for themselves—which was all anyone expected. But as church bells tolled vespers, peasants ranged through inns, homes, courtyards, even monasteries on the outskirts of town, looking for anyone foreign. Any who tried to hide, any who tried to run, any caught in disguise trying to get away, any who spoke with an accent

any who couldn't say "chickpea" like a Sicilian

was set upon by the mob and butchered.

Ed, I'm not being cynical, but, for me, looking back, the massacre of the French garrison isn't what stands out, any more than the certainty that some of those girlfriends turned informer (under the circumstances, that would be sensible, or else they were getting even). No, it's the idea that just when you think you're riding on top, the bed's upside down—and then even the commonplace can become the impossible.

Improvisation on Warhol's *Campbell's Soup Cans*

In SoHo, six years after this silkscreen's creation, one year
after the summer of love in San Francisco, Gretchen W., 19,
of Greenwich, theater-major, and Tony L., 20, also theater,
were murdered in a subdivided back bedroom of a crash pad.

After the summer of love in San Francisco, Gretchen W., 19,
decided that her life should be viewed on a stage with Tony:
that happened in a subdivided back bedroom in a crash pad,
with her body bloody and naked, face down on a mattress.

She'd decided her life should be viewed on a stage with Tony,
but that meant nothing to whomever it was who stabbed her,
leaving her body bloody and naked, face down on a mattress,
to be photographed by a NYC police forensics photographer.

But that meant nothing to whomever it was who stabbed her.
I don't remember if they caught him; I remember the girl's age.
To be photographed by a NYC police forensics photographer
was a terrible way to leave this world. I thought so then, still do.

I don't remember if they caught him. I remember the girl's age.
I was nineteen, seeing a Navy shrink, about to be discharged.
A terrible way to leave this world—thought so then, still do—
for Gretchen W., 19 and Tony L., 20—and for so many others.

Being assigned a shrink in boot camp guaranteed my discharge.
I'd signed up in the Navy just before I was about to be drafted.
For Gretchen W., 19 and Tony L., 20, and for so many others
their choices led them down their paths as mine led down mine.

I signed up just before being drafted, so many were drafted,
not knowing where it would lead, having only a few choices,
choices that led down one path or another, as mine did mine,
no one knowing where it would end, hoping it'd be different.

I'd read "The Road Not Taken"—all about choices, where each led—
like Tony L. under a window-security gate that was padlocked—
everyone choosing, one way or another, hoping it'd be different,
college or not, no choice alike, and all of it repeated over and over.

Tony L. chose the window whose security gate was padlocked
while Gretchen W. was found naked, face down on a bare mattress
in SoHo during the Vietnam War, when Warhol created a silkscreen,
soup cans like other soup cans, yet different, repeated over and over.

Nudes

Richard Avedon

The real shocker is the celebrity and not the nude.
Natassja Kinski with the boa constrictor is a pose.
Warhol and that band is anyone without clothes
until you see that it's Warhol there, and that goes
for Christy Turlington who's just a model from *Vogue*
until you know, or Ginsberg giving Orlovsky tongue,
or the young Nureyev in Paris, so alive, and hung.

Diane Arbus, Germaine Greer

Believe that this woman tasted her menstrual blood.
Or believed that western society existed to suppress
women and knew the means: to separate their sex
from them, leaving them fearful to be understood,
and, without men, nothing—*The Female Eunuch*—
from too much protein in urine in the preeclampsia
diagnosis, to Greer's portrait in Australia on a stamp.

Annie Leibovitz

Celebrity feeds upon everything and itself is food
and is never exhausted and is never satisfied,
finds pregnant Demi, ready to drop, in the nude
perfect for this occasion and only for this time;
if repeated (other naked Johns with Yokos), deified
in the original (thou shalt have one, not a multitude):
our burden, to know their future: her divorce, how he died.

Man Ray

The Classicism of solarized women posed as caryatids
holding up the temple; the Postmodernist droplets
dropped onto thighs before there was Photoshop;
the Surrealism of a nude woman becoming a cello
with F-holes, tail spike, belly, bridge, and pegbox;
Europe's exuberance after the Great War: batting eyelids,
fucking doggy-style, kewpie doll mouth sucking cock.

Edward Weston

The erotic is nowhere to be found in these tableaux,
There is nothing to suggest they eat, fuck, are capable
of birth, will die, be put into the ground and decompose.
Settings change: Hopi reservation, West as memorial
to some vanished myth that no one really has to know
(fake as a Wyeth *Saturday Evening Post* Thanksgiving table).
He did better showing erotic resemblances in vegetables.

Cindy Sherman

Disarticulated doll parts, like L.A.'s Black Dahlia
separated by several feet of grass in a vacant lot
(Elizabeth Short discarded like a mannequin in what
would become one of Hollywood's musts for film noir);
female doll heads, at a hacked plastic female torso, watch
a tampon string at bottom, a cock with cock ring at top:
clearly, woman objectified (and some men's darker desire).

R. Crumb

Someone in my generation would've drawn Snatch Comics
if he hadn't already, not only because of the weed shit
and LSD and free-love shit, but simply to see Crumb's us
with our heads disappearing up a woman's ass at a bus stop
(telling us to hurry because the bus is coming), or to catch
a hooker off-guard (saying "Excuse me" as we jiggle her clit)—
anything to keep away the jungle and napalm and the ditch.

Saving the Mare

We were both drunk driving back to the harness
track where my friend was a groom, with a sulky
and bunk, and who kept a notebook because he
was going to be a writer—but it was all business:
whenever he tried to write something in the barn
during a moment's down-time, it was interrupted
with mucking out a stall or getting horses watered,
or keeping an eye on the one with the bowed-tendon.
It wasn't fair, it wasn't fair, we whined to each other
as we had in Lost Angels (sliding bills under garters
so we could get close to the strippers); it wasn't fair
our jobs kept us from writing and no one cared—
like, with him, when the vet was up to his shoulders
inside the mare having cut in half her breached foal.

In Memoriam C. E. 1957–2014
At the Egyptian Museum of the Vatican

I followed a woman from one room into the next.
With light ahead, her dress became transparent.
What was she wearing? Was she pantyless?
I followed the woman from one room into the next.
She stopped at the foot of a female-faced sarcophagus
with gold-leaf and lapis for its final garment—
she wasn't its Ka appearing in this world from the next—
just a woman, with light ahead, her dress transparent.

Lewis Carroll Photographs of Alice Liddell

1. She's a street-urchin, standing against a wall
   overgrown with shrubbery (because it's her yard
   he's photographing her in; there's nothing hard
   in her appearance either, despite the clothes and all
   they're meant to suggest about her: more rags
   than clothes, she's a child of the streets who begs
   for her sustenance, when we know who really aches).

2. In this self-portrait with her, his face leans down
   to kiss her mouth, which he's helped turn up to his
   by guiding the prepubescent with his hand to kiss
   him—what does it matter if the entire world frown
   on their age difference if they love each other with all
   their hearts? This photo is a kind of marriage proposal.
   The Liddells may have broken with Dodgson over this.

3. Did he go down the rabbit hole? There are as many
   as a thousand photographic plates, say biographers,
   destroyed by him—some ask, how many were of her?
   There's a photo of Alice (not his), a woman of twenty,
   staring straight into the camera at us. You get a sense
   about something. (The Cheshire Cat would answer:
   absence of evidence is not evidence of absence.)

Sacred Flesh: Bonnard

1. *Nude in a Bath*

Some of the locations and objects and even the people
in his paintings are real, factual, like the cat on the table
prowling beside the glass of water or the pear on the dish,
but they do not exist in the present, which he submerges.
She looks up from the water in the tub knowing her image
in his mind is her from decades before; that's what his eye
sees. Marthe knows the present drowns; the past revives.

2. *Blue Nude*

Marthe is old—he's consumed with her: washing clothes;
when she sits at the table, wondering what to write next
in a letter; at breakfast, when spreading jam on her toast.
Here, in this painting, she is sitting on their bed after sex.
He tells her he smells her on his moustache, lips, fingers.
Even as he holds the paint brush, he tells the young poser,
he delights in her scent. (Marthe as ghost haunts the present.)

3. *The Bathroom*

When Renoir's hands, late in life, were so arthritic
that he could barely hold a brush, he was asked
by some young fool how he painted—*with my prick*,
he replied. Marthe accepts the lie: it is not the task
of the artist to represent life as it is, but the inner
life, even if not lived—he does not actually tell her
this, just as she does not tell her actual name: Maria.

4. *The Bathroom Mirror*

Marthe recognizes the porcelain bowl and pitcher
on the vanity, and the hairbrush and the perfume,
and knows what's reflected in the mirror isn't her,
just as the porcelain bowl isn't the bowl, the room
isn't the actual room (neither in the room reflected
in the mirror nor the foreground): the bowl shattered
decades ago—everything alive in the painting is dead.

5. *Nude Washing Feet in a Bathtub*

With left hand, she holds on to the bathtub rim
and lifts her left foot to wash it, watching him
out of the corner of her eye to see if he approves.
She feels the weight of her breasts, bending over.
She feels heel and arch and calluses at the bottom.
She feels the water's weight in the porcelain tub.
She feels the weight of years with this husband.

6. *The Toilet*

In the square of the vanity mirror, she is reflected,
so is the chair, so is the wallpaper; she's decapitated.
Only from her neck down to shins do we see her—
something like lotion in her hand, hair covering her vagina—
an art object contained in and framed by the mirror.
She knows this describes when, what and how he sees
the world. (After, she applies the lotion to her knees.)

7. Woman in Black Stockings

That is the past. The piece of juicy thigh showing.
Leg crossed over the other. Inspecting her stocking.
Breasts pendulous, exposed. Dressed in her undress.
Sitting at her vanity—when was it that she cared less
about material things and even her partial nakedness
got him hard and they'd fuck and that was enough?
When was it she began caring about other stuff?

8. Sombre Nude

This is the flesh but he doesn't see it. This
is the head bowed to the breasts bowing
down to the stomach folding into creases
above thighs that are closed and not opening
to receive him. This is the something not his
he cannot understand in the end is not hers.
He tells young Marthe, *Raise your head*; she does.

X-Factors: De Chirico

1. *The Melancholy of Departure*

The removal began precisely as its planners had decided
months earlier with names and ages and dispositions: dead,
the dispositions always showed those to be named dead
by execution or disease, and that too had been decided
in the planning—nothing was left to accident or chance,
with not so much as a question as to where the suitcases
would be piled on the platform (it took only a glance).

2. *The Disquieting Muses*

No one had time to open their mouths before they were gagged,
hooded, and set by the roadside. No matter how they begged,
it had no effect. Their heads were sewn shut like stuffed tailor
dummies. They had seen too much. In ancient Rome, a sailor
would have taken such violators (who had been sewn into a sack
for attempting to copy the Sibyl's texts), dropped them like rocks
into the sea for the fates they deserved, and never looked back.

3. *Love Song*

The surgeon's glove was pinned to the wall. He was a classicist
and had read Pliny, Polybius, Plutarch (of course) and missed
the republic before Caesar crossed the Rubicon. That was enough
to get him arrested (also his wife and his children). All of his stuff
was confiscated and was never seen again by anyone who knew it
was his (including his son's enormous green ball). All of this (and
more) was foretold in a memoir a decade before any of it happened.

4. The Melancholy and Mystery of a Street

His authority was absolute. In a flash, like a night camera
set up in the jungle of the Amazon (disguised on the floor
is the trip-wire), the girl was rolling a hoop toward a wagon
next to the building. His shadow watched. (In vast regions
of the Amazon, the panther's presence is only felt by humans.)
Questioned after the war about whether the girl still lived
and why he had followed her, the subject was unresponsive.

5. The Disquieting Muses

Two or three days passed. We stared at the hooded faces
like tailor dummies, in terrified silence, as if they were trying
to communicate with us. The factory alarm in the distance
signaled that it was time to return and that we were to bring
with us the ignorance of never having witnessed anything.
The scaffold reminded us of one hastily erected in Warsaw
which our guard marched us past, seeming to take forever.

6. The Enigma of the Hour

The clock in the bus station had stopped. In the square
the jurisdiction of the open space was disputed by doves.
It was like the quiet just before the minute hand moves.
A leaf, dry as ash, felt itself about to be swept into the air
but it did not stir. There were visible two shrouded figures,
and the silence was like that when there's nothing to say
because all had been said. The deportations began anyway.

7. The Nostalgia of the Infinite

It was, the orders said, an assembly point. Posted
everywhere, it was impossible not to have read
it, so it was impossible to ignore or not to obey.
Everyone was filled with trepidation. The day
finally arrived. Pennants on the tower waved
their goodbyes, until only two people were left.
To watch each hold the other's hand felt heroic.

8. Gare Montparnasse (The Melancholy of Departure)

Some decades later, a journalist profiled the couple,
beginning with the occupation at the start of the war,
how they saw train smoke, looked to the clock tower,
noted the time, and knew. In the newspaper article
they were portrayed as survivors of the impossible—
and the improbable detail. Being reunited took years.
(Only they saw bananas fall from the cart of a fruit vendor.)

View of the Paris Communard Dead Murdered by Versailles Troops at Père-Lachaise Cemetery, 1871

If this were El Salvador we'd guess they were leftists
or Sandinista border patrols surprised by Hondurans—
      but these numbered corpses,
a dozen men tagged and displayed in boxes,
were photographed to serve a different warning.
Still, the liver-colored blotches
of bullet wound, sepsis, and gas gangrene
seem all too familiar. . . .

Knowing that nothing like war so unites a people
      (including the petty German states)
      Bismarck outmaneuvered France
over claims to the Spanish throne's succession (July, 1870).
On Bastille Day, July 14*th*, the French mobilized.
Five days later war is declared—

in August, German victories—
    at Weissenburg, Worth, Spichern and Gravelotte.
By September, the Emperor Napoleon III surrenders at Sedan.
Paris that week declares a Republic—
it is encircled by German cannons still shining from foundries.
Adolphe Thiers, who heads the government—
and who will prove his worth to the monied interests—
acknowledges later that in continuing the siege
(from September through January)
"the object of our greatest concern *was insurrection.*"

How that government allowed near-starvation to become respectable
                    for the middle classes
is a success to be reckoned in truthfulness as well as order:
Encouraged by the wolf in the belly
showing its ribs,
boucheries, *canine et feline*,
sprang up without license at every corner.
Of which, semi-official pronouncements said
                chops of bulldog were "coarse and tasteless"
compared to leg of well-dressed poodle.
For the less affluent there were "gutter rabbits,"
Paris' prodigal and prolific cats
displayed with paper frills on doilies—
                        these to be garnished
with parsley, pistachio nuts, scallions, or radishes.
But for the starving masses, this was bread:
                flour and wallpaper paste,
                flour and straw,
                straw and water and wallpaper paste
                when there wasn't flour.
The poor queued along drains and gutters
                and fought for rats.

Of course, not everyone suffered,
                at least not so much.
Brokers at the Bourse still bought when rumors of armistice

panicked other profiteers and hoarders
(then bread and meat-tins became visible enough).
By December, some restaurants still could offer
        (for select diplomats and customers)
menus of Dwarf Zebra, Camel, Reindeer
        and the choice parts
        of two elephants
"only recently slaughtered for our patrons"
        at the Jardin des Plantes.

In the end (January), A. Thiers settled for an agreement
        secretly negotiated for months—
        war reparations
        and the occupation of Alsace—
but not until after one last bloody engagement
        (Buzenval) meant to save face.
(When, through inadvertence, the National Guard
        nearly accomplished a break-out,
        the government panicked.)

With capitulation, Bismarck was effusive—
        advising the French to first disarm
        their citizen "riffraff"
        and to "use the army"
(as events would prove later).
On March 1, at ten in the morning,

> Prussians in peaked helmets
> paraded down the Champs-Élysées
to a jeering Paris. . . .

How the city rose, how on the 18*th* the army went over
> (Thiers' government fleeing—
> it would return in two months),
abolishing the rents and overdue bills his crew had imposed
> (there's no limit to avarice);
who led them: how many shopkeepers, iron workers,
> seamstresses answered the cry
> for *pavés*—Paris' square
cobblestones erected as barricades—all and each
> have become part of the pantheon
> and folklore of slaughter:

> In a pen and ink cartoon
by Moloch, a decrepit Thiers pleads with Death
> to allow him time to use a cannon,
> aimed at Paris. The aged Chief Executive
is over seventy, he has one foot in the grave,
> and the skull of the Grim Reaper smiles
as it prepares to reap this harvest—

but it was the populations in the Rue de Rivoli, Invalides,
> and Montparnasse

which could not believe that Versailles troops
                would return in strength
                to bombard their city;
that the maimed and dying in makeshift hospitals
                would be bayoneted, along with doctors;
that women carrying bottles, accused as incendiaries,
                would be put to walls and instantly shot;
that in the last bloody week in May, *la semaine sanglante*,
                twenty-five thousand Parisians
                would be killed in the slaughter.
Of course, what the population refused to imagine
                was quickly accomplished.
On May 28*th*, this proclamation went out:

                INHABITANTS OF PARIS
                The French Army has come to your rescue.
                Paris is delivered. . . .

Months later, after the carnage,
Thiers offered that the Versailles had shown restraint,
                and reminded France
                and world opinion
that Communards had executed hostages—
                including officials, some Dominicans
                and the Archbishop of Paris.

Verlaine, later, nostalgic for bohème,
        would write of the flames'
        "horrible beauty";
Flaubert, incensed by all such
        "destroyers of property,"
wished all Communards "condemned to galleys";

and as for Paris' gorgeous boulevards
now so lovingly photographed
        with Dutch, Germans,
        Americans feeding pigeons,
these had been designed by Baron Georges-Eugène Haussmann
for Napoleon the Third
(nicknamed "the little")
to provide an unobstructed field for artillery.

⌣

45

Megapixels
Venice, 2005

When the Brothers of St. John the Decapitated
urged Giordano Bruno to recant, did they know
for certain that fire awaited, that an iron spike
would be driven through his tongue to stop up
his blasphemies once and for all? Picture
someone doing that; then picture an iron gag

already locking his jaw in place, meant to gag
him, screwed with such force it would decapitate
a person less hard-headed. And now picture
a second spike, driven into his palate. Bruno
was aware. He'd been tortured for years to give up
all of those heresies of his, which were as a spike

driven into the heart of the Church, a spike
it couldn't remove, that made it writhe and gag
and foam. And one heresy he wouldn't give up,
that he faced being burned alive for, not decapitated,
which would have been merciful? Bruno didn't know
how a woman conceived without sex. (Picture

the Church hearing that.) Bruno could picture
a Copernican universe, not that. (Another spike!)
It didn't make sense. It defied reason. Bruno

believed in reason, in the mind, so he was gagged.
Given a choice, to be burned alive or decapitated,
other reasonable people would have given up

their beliefs. Giovanni Mocenigo gave him up.
I'm passing Giovanni's palace, taking pictures.
Giovanni also feared the Inquisition. Decapitate
Bruno, or burn him as a witch with iron spikes
driven through his tongue and palate to gag
him once and for all—Giovanni didn't need to know.

Account-books of his trials in Rome list Bruno's
expenses, including rope, fresh saplings piled up
so he burned slowly, the two spikes and iron gag
that stopped his blasphemies. I'm taking pictures.
On the news this morning, there was another spike
in killings in Iraq, with more workers decapitated.

A deckhand ties up our water-bus to a metal spike.
I'm on vacation. I know I'm not good at taking pictures.
I know it makes people gag the way I decapitate things.

Crossing Sartre's Bridge with Inez and Estelle during the Iraq War

Venice, 2005

I found myself standing at the top of a bridge—
　　　　really, little more than stone steps
arched over a narrow secondary canal—to watch

half a dozen gondolas and canal barge traffic
　　　　get backed up. There was no exit.
There was nothing anyone could do. Nothing.

A small barge was jammed sideways. Nothing
　　　　the driver did could free it. From the bridge
you could see part of the problem· with no exit,

those behind pushed forward, though on the steps
　　　　people shouted it was blocked, that traffic
couldn't go anywhere. On the wall, kids watched,

waved to their friends to come over. They watched—
　　　　laughing, poking fun—because nothing
the guy did, like push against a hull the traffic

pushed into his barge, made a difference. On the bridge
　　　　more people came to watch. The bridge's steps
filled with people, many shouting, others silent. It

was surreal. It made me think of Sartre's *No Exit*—
　　　　people without eyelids forced to watch
but not understanding anything. On the steps

this one woman—there was really nothing
          special about her, she was on the bridge—
she just stood there and stared down at the traffic,

at this one gondola, wedged in by the traffic,
          being slowly pushed forward until it
bumped a boat stacked with Coca-Cola. On the bridge

the Italian woman waved to the gondola. I watched.
          An American woman shouted to her, nothing
that made sense, I'm sure, to the woman on the steps—

about seeing the Colosseum, the Spanish Steps,
          Trevi Fountain, the horrendous traffic
everywhere in Rome, the Vatican—but nothing

about Venice—and she was stuck in the middle of it.
          Not one word about Saint Marks. She watched
the woman above her nodding from the low bridge.

That night on the BBC, I heard Bush talking *necessary steps—exit*
          strategy—Al-Qaeda—watch list—insurgents who traffic
in death. I understood nothing. I was on that bridge.

Apocalypse
Rome, April 2006

Three Italian soldiers and one Rumanian
      have been blown up by a roadside bomb
in Iraq. It's all over the news. Italy was supposed to be withdrawing

her troops from what most Italians feel
      is a manufactured war, which they wanted
no part of, and didn't from the beginning—

but the people weren't listened to. Beginning
      now, maybe they will be—unlike the Rumanian
woman begging at the end of the line: she wanted

her poverty to be believed, but her cup was empty. The bomb
      was an IED, like those killing our troops. I feel
strange standing in line at the Vatican—there's a girl drawing

the statues that line the top of St. Peter's. It's a charcoal drawing.
      The line goes all the way back, beginning
with the saw-horses that are set up just inside the plaza. It feels

odd. This morning, the Danube was overflowing and Rumanian
      farmers were sandbagging levees that look bombed.
The dirt roads were filled with horse-drawn wagons. I wanted

to get away from the news, but you don't always get what you want,
      as Mick says. The girl isn't wearing a bra. She's drawing
statues of saints, the levees look like they were bombed

by Stukas, and I'm peeking through an armhole. At the beginning
        of this line waiting to get into the Vatican there's a Rumanian
woman begging. How's that for a confluence? If she feels

like every one of us is a prick, she's right, because I feel
        nothing for her. I saw one of her in Venice. I wanted
to get past her to the train station. I was in a hurry. The Rumanian

countryside is under water. Italy was supposed to be withdrawing
        from Iraq and three of her soldiers got killed by a bomb
inside an animal carcass. That's what it said in the beginning

of the news segment this morning. I was just beginning
        to have breakfast in the dining room of my hotel (I don't feel
like myself until I have coffee) when news of the roadside bomb

was all they could talk about. It was like being back home. I wanted
        to get away—and then there was Bush saying, "Withdrawing
our troops prematurely would be a mistake." The Rumanian

who got killed by that bomb was hardly mentioned. I wanted
        to see the Sistine Chapel. I feel odd. There's a girl drawing.
At the beginning of the line there's a woman I think is Rumanian.

On Guido Reni's *Apollo Flaying Marsyas* as Iraq

As Auden once said, there's nothing abstract
about suffering if you pay attention.
In this painting, for example, torture is fact:
Apollo kneels into Marsyas' groin and begins.

Marsyas is suffering. If you pay attention
you can almost hear this victim
as Apollo kneels into his groin and begins.
Look at his mouth: Nothing comes out of him.

You can almost hear this victim
but you don't—pain makes sound disappear.
Look at his mouth: Nothing comes out of him.
The knife cuts into bone, but his fear

dissolves humanity, not pain. Sound disappears.
As Auden once said, there's nothing abstract
about suffering. Look at his mouth. Hear
in his silence all victims. Torture is fact.

Boxes

It's a shell game which involves finding the pea
          under one of three small cardboard boxes
that the con artist and his hidden accomplice

in the crowd have worked to perfection.
          In Rome's metro, there were posters
everywhere warning tourists about the flimflam.

This was summer, 2003, and the Iraq flimflam
          about WMD hidden somewhere, unlike that pea
under the princess' mattresses, had worked. Posters

had been put up everywhere promising boxes
          of cash for Iraqis to find them. It was perfection.
Every night, our news media were accomplices

to the fraud as they made us accomplices,
          wondering how Saddam pulled off his flimflam
of hiding such weapons. Like I said, perfection.

Saddam was playing a shell game, hiding the pea,
          and just when we thought we had him in a box—
because he was also the pea, and posters

of him had gone up everywhere, posters
          promising fortunes for him and his accomplices
(his sons Uday and Qusay, who turned up in boxes)—

all of us were conned again and again by the flimflam
            of him, like those weapons, suddenly (like a pea)
disappearing from one shell to under another. Perfection.

You've got to admit, it was worked to perfection.
            I was riding the Rome metro, staring at posters
warning me about the "Three Boxes and the Pea"

and to be on my guard for the con and his accomplice
            because they would be expert at the flimflam
and I'd never find the pea under the right box—

but that only made me think of other boxes
            coming home from a war and the perfection
of the lies told to everyone then, only that flimflam

involved rice paddies. Spray-painted subway posters
            demanded that LBJ, and McNamara, his accomplice,
explain why more and more had to die to have peace.

I was strap-hanging, simultaneously in two hotboxes, with posters
            warning of perfect cons that made people accomplices
to flimflams, to shell games, whenever they tried to follow the pea.

A Pipe

"Ceci n'est pas une pipe"—this is not a pipe:
that's the meaning of the phrase Magritte painted
under the pipe in his painting—or, what we see
may not be what really is, defying us to figure out
what really is from what we may think we know,
suggesting it makes a difference or doesn't matter.

My first time in Paris, a lifetime ago, it didn't matter
where I slept—on the ile de Saint Louis, the pipes
rattled with every flush in the hall, and I didn't know
a door latch made the light go on in a toilet painted
with such pornographic graffiti I couldn't figure out
which organ was going into which—all I could see

was some long tube entering some tunnel, or else see
a snake being swallowed. Why a snake? It didn't matter
why because the point, of course, wasn't to figure it out.
There was a war going on in Asia, and like Magritte's pipe
it wasn't. It was and it wasn't. Like that phrase painted
beneath the pipe, you knew what you didn't want to know.

I was still in my teens, married, and didn't want to know.
I'd just been discharged from the reserves. I didn't see
my draft notice coming. It could have been painted
on my forehead in a mirror and it wouldn't matter,
so I signed up to avoid service. Like Magritte's pipe,
signing up in the military to avoid a war kept me out.

It was a piece of shit hotel. My wife and I stayed out
all night just to avoid going back to it. We didn't know
who we were or where we were headed. Like that pipe,
we were what we appeared and what we couldn't see.
Even had it been pointed out, it wouldn't have mattered.
Our lives were real, and weren't, like a pipe in a painting.

And still are real and unreal, but they aren't a painting
and what has happened over their course has turned out
well (I'll speak for me) because my two children matter,
my wife, brother, friends, and the poems I've read and know
they matter though I couldn't tell you how: everyone will see
what they see, in this poem or any other poem, like that pipe.

It is what it is, what it appears, and isn't, in a painting we know
is a painting—something we can try to figure out, or simply see.
Maybe it does matter. Maybe it doesn't. It's a phrase. It's a pipe.

'60s Fellini Noir

They came to the East Village during the Summer of Love.
The police found their bodies in the back room of a crash pad.
She was face down on a bare mattress; he was by a window.
Another window onto the fire escape was gated and padlocked.

The police found their bodies in the back room of the crash pad.
Downstairs, braless girls painted like Indians danced to bongos.
Several NYPD vehicles blocked off both ends of the street.
I was in uniform then, trying to get discharged from the service.

Downstairs, braless girls painted like Indians danced to bongos.
Face down, stabbed repeatedly, her blood soaked into the mattress.
He tried to flee to the fire escape but the window-gate was padlocked.
My psychiatrist couldn't promise me more than a general discharge.

Face down, stabbed repeatedly, her blood soaked the mattress.
He had his jeans on, no shirt; there were stab wounds to his chest.
Late newspaper editions ran their photos with stories of the murders.
Above the folds were stories about the war and more troop escalations.

He was shirtless, slumped in a corner, with stab wounds to his chest.
Several NYPD vehicles had blocked off both ends of the street.
My psychiatrist couldn't promise me more than a general discharge.
That girl and boy came to the East Village during the Summer of Love.

Regrets, No Regrets
the Viking Danube Cruise

1.

She sings Piaf, "Non, je ne regrette rien,"
(Oscar already introduced at the piano,
who nodded behind her), "La vie en rose,"
"Hymne à l'amour," "La Foule," and then
it's on to others, mixing biography in,
starting with Piaf's name as nickname ("sparrow");
father, an acrobat; grandmother running a brothel;
blindness from keratitis from age three to seven;
her miraculous recovery; and then, quickly,
accused as an accessory to her nightclub owner's
murder, but acquitted; accused of being a traitor
during the war—and the lounge is almost empty.
She barely mentions, in a whisper, Charles Aznavour;
asks we tell the entertainment director if we approve.

2.

She sang Piaf's "Non, je ne regrette rien,"
one leg crossed over the other on the piano,
showing lots of thigh for one whose blush was off the rose
but then what did any of it matter—sing, then
get paid, but throw some autobiography in—
her father, the war—breadcrumbs to sparrows
when the veterans hear that (not the brothel
divided-Berlin became after, until she was seven,
when the West German miracle quickly

became economic juggernaut: owners
on one side of the wire, on the other side traitors);
the only pause is when her martini glass is empty.
She mentioned her name (I remember Charles Aznavour),
asked we tell the entertainment director if we approved.

3.

She sings Piaf's "Non, je ne regrette rien,"
no regrets, and looks back to "Oscar on piano"
whose faint smile back to her is the single rose
anyone will hand her on this stage; then
it's a short hop down onto the dance floor, in
black satin, to work the crowd, "little sparrow"
not so little, someone you'd see in a brothel-
window years past, not today's websites (seven
thumbnails beneath a large spread-shot, quickly
replaced—with each mouse click, you own her).
She pinches a cheek, but memory is the real traitor:
TV, that stiff Irishman trying to make empty
banter with the short frenchie, Charles Aznavour,
singing Piaf on *Ed Sullivan*—my mother approves.

4.

She sang Piaf, "Non, je ne regrette rien,"
a German, older than I am, sitting on a piano
drinking dirty martinis stirred with an olive, rose
to give us a history of Piaf's loves before war, then
after, and some of her own biography (West Berlin,
as a little girl, hopping around, not like a sparrow
to hopscotch-lines chalked on sidewalk, but brothel-
change thrown like candy when she's six or seven—
the German "economic miracle" coming quickly,
not quickly enough), and all the while, listening to her,
I'm thinking of my veteran father—his mind, traitor;
receiving convulsive shock until his brain was empty—
my mom watching that suave frenchie Charles Aznavour.
That's life, and it doesn't matter whether you approve.

Nuremberg
July, 2013

1.

After you pay the museum admission, the woman
goes over to the headphone sets on the counter
and motions you to put one on: you'll look at her
as you wait for her to switch the audio from German—
and that's what you'll see them all do (Hermann
especially, in the video, the puffed-up dandy who prefers
his own death sentence, a cyanide ampule after dinner);
because that's what they all do, every one—to a man,
they wait for the translation to come into the headset
and they stare out in front of them, as if into the future:
they're waiting for that future to suddenly materialize
into the language of the past—and when they get
what they feel entitled to, some put on the disguise
of being someone interested in the words of others.

2.

But others don't pretend—in the hall video, the woman
on the witness stand takes the headphones on the counter,
puts them on and looks at the judge, who looks at her
to see whether she understands German—
and when she indicates she does, you see Hermann
at the end of the aisle, the bulk of him, ignore
the woman's voice with his attempted after-dinner
chat to the criminal next to him in the dock—a man,
unlike himself, who listens to the voice in his headset

as if that voice were a diviner's telling his future:
words adding to puzzle, whole beginning to materialize,
pressing ear-piece with fingertips in order to get
every nuance, head suddenly dropping, his disguise
falling away—he is no different from the others.

3.

Next to me, watching the video, a young woman
takes her son's headset (who fidgeted on the counter
with several before taking this one and looked at her
wide-eyed as his mother scolded him in German);
the boy's headset's not working— overripe Hermann,
who's lost weight, making him seem shabby, encounters
the mom's annoyance at her son with an after-dinner
picking of his teeth with a thumbnail—he is a man
used to having what he wants, not a voice in a headset
whose owner always looks back, not to the future,
a better future, he suspects, that can still materialize—
but not, just as in Greek myth, by looking back—you get
what you deserve by doing that (ever cultivated—Göring's disguise).
The exasperated mom and son leave to get another headset.

4.

I understand that boy, I understand that young woman's
anger, her son not doing what she wants—going counter
to her wishes—my son teased his sister, teased her

unrelentingly; you didn't need to understand German
to know what she said—or to understand Hermann
as he keeps drumming his fingers on the counter
as victim after victim testifies and spoils his supper
that will be served to him later in his cell—by a man,
Göring would argue, no different from himself, headset
or no headset, or those taking poison, fearing the future
rather than taking their chances, waiting for it to materialize—
like himself—who doesn't believe the death sentence he gets
(the cyanide ampule finally unmasks Göring's disguise).
The exasperated mom and kid return with another headset.

5.

This suddenly happened—some old, naked female
human being who would soon be shot on the order
of a German with a horse crop who stood apart
from another Nazi with a dog whose gums were merlot-
colored, his fangs bared. Concentration camp photo art.
Nuremberg. In color. You didn't have to be a mind-reader
to know what was going on in each picture either; you're
following the translator's voice in your headset, each spot
number-coded on the wall to your handset. Nowhere
to get lost: punch the number into the handset, you lock
into the recording telling you all about the photo. You stop
or move on as you want because it's not timed. In Vienna
this guy on our cruise nodded off during the symphony, as in Budapest.
Here, he was crying, couldn't stop, in front of human spines like fish.

Looking at the Göring Suicide Photograph
Nuremberg Museum, 2013

The drug my older brother took made his tongue swell
out of his mouth, thick as a cow's tongue, but immoveable.
It was either court-ordered medication or jail—

with a short stretch in Saint Vincent's, arranged by the cardinal;
my mother was a cook for the archdiocese, knew people,
and one of the monsignors had pull.

(If there was a next time, it wouldn't be Ward's Island hospital,
no matter what the household conditions were or how troubled
the individual   the next time would be jail.)

My younger brother didn't know anything—he was a child,
grew up doing the ordinary, neighborhood stuff: pills,
weed, beer, but not, thankfully, the heroin that made his friends ill.

And me. Thorazine. Let me sleep-walk through fire damage control
in basic, helped carry my tray in line at the mess hall,
and steadied my weapon in the one-time-only drill

that forty six years later I can hardly recall,
But I remember this photo   Göring's lazy eye, the ampule
of cyanide crushed between his teeth not visible.

I remember it in place of my father's funeral.
I wasn't there. He died in Florida, after electro-
convulsive shock and years in-and-out of VA hospitals

and home visits and restraining orders he ignored at his peril
and of which I have no memory at all.
I remember a suitcase in a hall closet with V-mail.

And this photo in magazines. Göring on his back in his cell—
how strange seeing it again, here, and the black-and-white trial
photos, and, in the dock, all of those old war criminals.